# TABLE of CONTENTS

*To my wife, Raquel*
*–source of inspiration and driving force that*
*keeps me moving forward.*

# Introduction

You may be wondering why somebody would write a book about Database Administration when there are in the market more books than anybody can read about Oracle, DB2, SQL Server, Sybase, etc. Here is why: because this book addresses Database Administration independently of the technology of choice.

Over the years I noticed some questions about databases in general, and database administration in particular are asked once and again; actually, many years ago I asked those questions myself.

At first, I was under the impression that that kind of questions would be asked by fresh entry level Database Administrators. However, to my surprise, they keep popping up and are asked by both inexperienced and experienced database professionals as well as by management and professionals from other Information Technology and Information Systems domains like Software development, Systems, Data compliance, Project management, etc.

Bottom line is that people keep asking what are the responsibilities of a Database

Administrator, what are the specific tasks and processes Database Administrators rely on to fulfill those responsibilities and, by which rules Database Administrators abide to deal with whatever they do.

Some people ask those questions out of simple curiosity, others because they are in or close to a DBA role, others because they have to deal with DBAs – in a user, developer, management, etc. capacity, and want to have a better understanding of the DBA community.

Everyone has its own reasons to ask questions about the database world; questions are always the same.

This book intends to answer those questions.

As implied before, the target audience is not only Database Administrators but also other Information Technology and Information Systems professionals ranging from entry level to management level that may benefit from better understanding what Database Administrators do, why they do it and, how they do it – all of these without entering in technicalities and independently of the technology of choice.

# About The Author

**Pablo Berzukov** is a Senior Database Administrator with in excess of a quarter century of hands-on Information Technology industry experience. He has worked for corporations and governmental agencies in the United States and overseas; he is a published author.

His IT career started as an Assembly programmer, had the opportunity to work with the pioneers of online and database systems, witnessed the rise of relational databases, worked as an Applications Programmer, Systems Programmer, Functional Analyst, Systems Analyst, Project Manager and Consultant being the Database domain a recurrent focus area throughout his career.

Mr. Berzukov holds a Bachelor of Science degree in Information Technology Management as well as several industry certifications from Oracle, Microsoft and CompTia. He is a MBA candidate. For up-to-date information check his personal LinkedIn profile at www.linkedin.com/in/PabloBerzukov

## Acknowledgments

Illustrations on this book are clipart by clker.com according to the terms described at www.clker.com/disclaimer.html under *creative public domain license* policies documented at creativecommons.org/licenses/publicdomain/

This book is built from the experience of the author but also on the experience of many others who over the years shared their knowledge and personal opinions. Thank you all.

## Trademarks

Oracle, IBM, Microsoft, Sybase and other corporate names as well as Oracle, DB2, SQL Server, Sybase an others products names, brands, trademarks, etc. are mentioned in this book solely for referential purposes. The use of any of those terms in this book should not be regarded as affecting the validity of any trademark or service mark.

## Disclaimer

Every effort has been made to make this book as complete and accurate as possible but no warranty is implied. All information in this book is provided in an "as is" basis. The author and publisher shall have neither liability nor responsibility to any person or entity with respect to any loss or damage arising from the information contained in this book.

## Feedback and Contact

Feedback and other comments on this book can be sent to RnP_Books@live.com – please include the book's title in the subject line.

The same address can be used to contact the author who monitors the abovementioned mailbox on a best effort basis.

# Chapter 1
# Let's Get Started

Chapter 1 - Road Map

- Understanding how this book was designed.

- Meet your host: Jason.

- Meet Jason's friend, an old hand DBA.

Chapter 1

Let's Get Started

"Introducing Jason and how this book works"

## About Jason

This book is about answering questions, therefore, we are in need of somebody willing to ask those questions and keep hammering until getting the right answers; with no further ado let me introduce you: Jason!

Jason is a very important character in this book –only second to you, he is the one that would guide you throughout this book; he is also the one that will ask all those questions about databases and database administration.

Who is Jason? What does he do?

Jason, an old friend of mine is a [*Jason's_Title*] trying to figure it out what Database Administrators really do.

My suggestions for *Jason's_Title* are:

- Auditor
- College student
- Consultant
- C level person
- Director
- Entry level Database Administrator
- Functional analyst
- Help desk associate or manager
- Manager
- Network engineer
- Project Manager
- Quality assurance engineer
- Software engineer
- Storage administrator
- Systems administrator

- Whatever other position comes to your mind.

## The Importance of Having an Inner Circle Contact

As you will see, Jason is a very curious person and most important he is being blessed by having a close friend who is an experienced Database Administrator.

Why is that so important? Because sometimes over the phone, sometimes over instant messenger, and, other times walking a golf course, Jason has the opportunity to ask his friend everything that comes to his mind about what Database Administrators really do, why they do it and, how they do it.

## Tips

| Aha! | *"Aha!" boxes are used to highlight specific concepts.* |
|------|------------------------------------------------------------|
| D B A corner | *"DBA corner" boxes are used to share information with DBA reading this book.* |

## Technology Agnostic

This is a technology agnostic book meaning that it applies to the field of database administration in general rather than focusing on any specific database vendor technology in particular.

The final intention is to help you understand the world of Database Administration without resorting to technicalities, independently of the technology of choice and, without a single SQL command.

Appendix I include definitions for all technical terms used in this book in the form of a Dbaish-English dictionary.

Enjoy the ride.

# Chapter 2

# Database Administration beyond Technology

Chapter 2 - Road Map

- Looking into what a DBA does.

- Background information about database technologies.

- DBA responsibilities at a glance.

- DBA and specific database technologies.

- The database market.

Chapter 2

Database Administration beyond
Technology

"Where Jason shows an interest in
knowing about database administration"

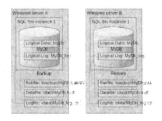

## Looking for the Answer to the

## Ultimate Question

From now on allow me to refer to Database
Administrators as DBA, if you are an
experienced DBA feel free to skip this short
chapter – no harm if you decide to stay.

Oops... give me a second please, an instant
messenger window just popped up on my
laptop.

[JasonQ] r u there?
[oldDBA] yes I'm
[JasonQ] cool...
[JasonQ] what's different between Oracle and SQL Server DBA?
[JasonQ] ... do they do different things?
[oldDBA] they do the same things...
[oldDBA] probably in different ways...
[oldDBA] I'll tell you, do you have a sec?

I think it was James T. Mccay who said "one good analogy is worth three hours discussion" so let me approach this question with an analogy.

Database technology comes from different vendors like Oracle, IBM (DB2), Microsoft (SQL Server) and so on; the same way cars come from different manufacturers like Ford, GM, Toyota, and so on. All are different but at the same time all are the same – just a different spin on the same basic idea.

All cars no matter the manufacturer come with a frame, engine, wheels, etc. and, are designed to move people; some are automatic, some are manual, some burn gas, some are hybrid, but those are just flavors or different features over the same basic idea that make one or other car more or less efficient or more or less attractive to customers in certain conditions or scenarios.

Let me show you how the same happens in the database world.

## Some Background Information

No matter who is the vendor of your database system – generically called RDBMS which stands for **R**elational **D**ata **B**ase **M**anagement **S**ystem, all of them are based in the same basic idea which is the Relational Theory.

The relational theory can be traced back to June 1970 when Dr. E. F. Codd published a paper entitled "A Relational Model of Data for Large Shared Data Banks".

In a world dominated by database systems based on *network* and *hierarchic* models the idea was revolutionary. People started to work looking to build a working database system based on such *relational* model.

Arguable the first –or one of the earliest commercially available relational database management systems, was Adabas back in 1971. It took years before *relational* database technology improved performance beyond what databases based on *network* and *hierarchical* models were able to provide.

You may want to think on databases in an evolutionary way, *network* and *hierarchical* database technologies dominated the world for a period of time; then *relational* databases appeared, evolved, got faster, more reliable and took over.

Looking at the big picture all RDBMS do the same, they allow to administer storage space, have the ability to store and retrieve data, provide means to take backups and recover in case something goes wrong, all rely in buffering data in memory for performance purposes, all rely in locking to protect the integrity of the data, all support physical implementation of third normal form data models and beyond, all of them currently *talk* some flavor of SQL language, etc.

On the other hand all of them have differences like some cars are automatic while others are manual; some burn gas while others are hybrids. Remember?

| | |
|---|---|
| **Aha!** | *All modern relational database systems like IBM-DB2, Oracle, Microsoft SQL Server, etc. are different developments of the same basic idea... the relational theory!* |

# DBA Responsibilities are always the Same

Let me attempt a summarization. Since all implementations of the relational model originally proposed by Mr. Codd e.g. all RDBMS on the market today allow to do the same things – manage storage space, store and retrieve data, etc. – then all DBA should do more or less the same things no matter which RDBMS they are working on.

[oldDBA] are you following so far?
[JasonQ] sort of...
[JasonQ] please complete the rdbms-car analogy
[oldDBA] there we go

Bottom line is that an average DBA has to learn how to handle a given database engine the same way a driver has to learn how to drive a given car. A DBA knows what the gas and brake pedals are for, may be she/he would need to get acquainted with other controls in the panel but they do not have to learn about the whole concept of having four wheels attached to a frame, an engine, etc. because all database engines are somehow alike –like cars are.

The responsibilities of a DBA do not change depending on the vendor of the database. Some database technologies are half siblings like Microsoft SQL Server, Sybase and MySQL are; others are second degree cousins like Oracle and IBM DB2 but, under more or less layers of technicalities, all of them go back to the same original concept.

| | |
|---|---|
| **Aha!** | *No matter what the underlying technology is, e.g. Oracle, SQL Server, Sybase, DB2, Informix, MySQL, etc., Database Administrator responsibilities are always the same because all RDBMS are based on the same concept!* |

## Having Said That

Having said that let me make a very important note: it takes years of training and hands-on experience for a good DBA to master a specific technology e.g. Oracle, DB2, SQL Server, etc.

The same way nobody expects an average commuter driver to be able to match the skills of an average Nascar driver ten minutes after sitting in the car, nobody should expect a DBA to master the technology of other vendor in a split second. In the DBA world experience matters big time.

Just to be sure Jason and I are on the same page let me say it one more time: the responsibilities of a DBA are the same no matter the technology vendor but, specific skills set and hands on experience are a very different story.

| | |
|---|---|
| ***Aha!*** | *Oracle, SQL Server, Sybase, DB2, MySQL, etc. are different implementations of the same underlying concept, therefore DBA responsibilities are the same. However, DBA have to master specific skills depending on the technology vendor!* |

## DBMS Market

[JasonQ] mmmhhh... ok; I think I got it.
[JasonQ] you mention different database vendors...
[JasonQ] how is market share nowadays?
[oldDBA] ball park numbers?

There are several database vendors in the market ranging from power houses like Oracle,

IBM and Microsoft to what we can call *small shops* and even "royalty free" products like MySQL and PostgreSQL but, the bulk of the market is dominated by a few ones. Ball park numbers are as follows:

| Data Base Management System | Market Share |
|---|---|
| Oracle | 44.5% |
| IBM-DB2 | 21.0% |
| Microsoft SQL Server | 18.5% |
| Sybase | 3.5% |
| Teradata | 3.5% |
| Others | 9.0% |

It is interesting to note that from the point of view of the platforms on top of which databases are implemented there are three different market segments, those are:

- Traditional Mainframe machines,
- Unix/Linux alike machines and,
- Windows machines.

Even when Oracle is the overall dominant force of the database market, each one of these markets segments has it own champion: IBM-DB2 is the champion of the traditional mainframe segment, SQL Server has a tiny lead in the Windows segment and Oracle is the power house of the Unix/Linux market segment.

On the other hand, there are vendors attempting to segment the market in a different way to take advantage of different market niches. In general vendors sell a RDBMS for general purposes, meaning you can manage any type of database. In this context *any kind* means databases that support OLTP processes and databases that support Data Warehousing and Business Intelligence processes.

As an example, one vendor in particular - Teradata, offers a "specialty" RDBMS designed to address the Data Warehousing market.

# Chapter 3
# What does a DBA Do?

Chapter 3 Road Map

- A first approach to DBA responsibilities.

- Learn about database Integrity, Availability, Recoverability, Performance and Security.

Chapter 3

What does a DBA do?

"Where the discussion gets to specifics"

## A Frustrating Question

[JasonQ] mmmhhh... ok; got that but...
[JasonQ] what does a DBA do?
[oldDBA] DBAs administer databases ☺

The problem with the answer is that the
answer is embedded in the question; it is neat,
clear and at the same time most probably
does not answer what the person who asked
the question really wants to know. Chances
are the person who asked the question wanted
to know what a DBA does all day long other
than peppering conversations with words like

"table", "row", "column", "normalization", "replication" and even "tuple", "non-sargable" and others of the sort.

Most people stop asking questions at this point, let's see what Jason does.

## Let's Ask a Different Question

[JasonQ] funny guy... let me rephrase...
[JasonQ] what are the responsibilities of a DBA?
[oldDBA] good job! lol
[oldDBA] DBAs are responsible for database integrity, availability, recoverability, performance and security.
[JasonQ] No matter if it's Oracle, Sybase or whatever?
[oldDBA] correct! You got it

That was a much better question; it forces an answer that points to specifics allowing for follow up questions that have the potential of drilling down details of what really happens in the DBA world.

## Database Integrity

[JasonQ] so... DBAs are responsible for data integrity?
[JasonQ] great!
[JasonQ] now I know whom to call when a phone number shows wrong on some customer report...
[JasonQ] Thank you!!!
[oldDBA] Hey! ... Not that fast my friend...

[oldDBA] database integrity is not the same as data quality ☺
[JasonQ] WHAT?!... Tell me more...
[oldDBA] let me tell you...

Database Integrity means DBAs are responsible for keeping data in the database as it was stored but DBAs are not responsible for the quality of the data itself; DBAs takes care of the packaging, users are responsible for the content.

Let me say it again, DBAs are responsible for the Integrity of the Database as a whole but DBAs own neither the data nor the code a.k.a. programs. This is a very important concept and we will come back to it later.

Users are responsible for the data; application team, or whatever the software development team is called in your organization, is responsible for the code.

[oldDBA] so... if you see "bad" data you have to call both the user and the developers...
[oldDBA] ...looking to figure it out if the "bad" data comes from a human error or a program error...
[oldDBA] we DBAs will be happy to help but we do not "own" the issue...
[oldDBA] got it? ☺

It is not an unseen event that the first person to be called or paged when a user finds "bad data" is a DBA.

The DBA will help determine if the data is actually "bad" or if is just showing wrongly in the affected screen or report but, once a determination has been made about the root cause of what the user sees as "bad data", most likely other people have to be involved.

Case 1: Data is fine in the database but shows bad in a report or screen. In this case the Development team needs to be involved. If data shows bad in a screen or report but it is fine in the database, the only possible reason would be an application related issue.

Case 2: Data is not good in the database and as a result, it shows bad in a report or screen. In this case the User and the Development team have to be involved. If data is bad in the database, that means a program or person put it there the way it shows. User and Developer should figure out if a program is creating the problem or if a User made a mistake.

| | |
|---|---|
| **Aha!** | *Database Integrity is not the same as Data Quality, users own the data, and therefore, they are responsible for the quality of the data.* |

## Database Availability

[JasonQ] mmmhhhkay... I think I got it, how about availability?
[oldDBA] let me put it this way...

DBAs are responsible for making database available to the users at least to fulfill the terms of the Service Level Agreement a.k.a. SLA, agreed with the Business for each specific database.

Not all databases have to be available all the time, not all databases have the same SLA.

Some databases support activities that happen from Monday through Friday from 9 to 5, therefore most probably those databases will have an SLA stating that they have to be available from Monday through Friday from 9 to 5, while other critical databases that have to be available 24 hours a day would have SLAs stating that.

In the case of critical databases, like a database supporting an online reservations or online sales system, the Business may want to have in place Disaster Avoidance protocols – usually called Business Continuity Plans, that in case of a "disaster" on the primary site would switch activity from the primary to a secondary database usually located in a remote location.

Please note that the operational cost of operating a database that needs to be available from Monday through Friday from 9 to 5 is going to be much less expensive that the cost of operating a database that needs to be available 24 by 7 and even with the ability to continue operations in a secondary location if "disaster" hits the primary location.

[JasonQ] why would I bother in having different SLA?
[JasonQ] Let's have a single SLA for all databases...
[JasonQ] like all of them available 24 by 7
[oldDBA] you are not listening...
[oldDBA] There is a reason why not... money!!!
[oldDBA]The more "uptime" you want on your SLA the more expensive the operation of that particular database would be.
[JasonQ] you have a point there... who decides SLA?
[oldDBA] Business does... let me tell you how

The first step in the process of setting an SLA is to sort out which databases deserve which treatment. Since it has to be cost effective, it is based on how critical a specific database is for the operation – or even the survival, of the organization.

SLAs usually go hand-in-hand with Disaster Recovery, also known as Business Continuity planning. In terms of business survivability, Corporations usually organize systems and databases in three categories, which in simple terms are:

- Database can be down for a week.
- Database can be down for a couple of days.
- Cannot live without this database.

DBAs usually work alongside Systems administrators and other teams advising Business in regards to SLA, however, the ultimate decision in that sense is made by Business.

Just as a side note, please note that SLA usually includes "maintenance windows" meaning time slots where certain databases are not going to be available to the users. Those windows are designed to allow DBAs, Systems administrators and other teams to perform whatever tasks are needed to ensure the good health of the target system.

| **Aha!** | *The expected availability of a database depends on the Service Level Agreement for that specific database; usually based on criticality!* |
|---|---|

## Database Recoverability

[JasonQ] I see…
[JasonQ] … is "availability" somehow related to
"recoverability"?
[oldDBA] yes … and, no ☺

It is clear that the final intend of recovering a
damaged database is to make it available but
we prefer to treat the recoverability issue as a
separate one.

Recoverability is directly related to backup and
recovery strategy. And guess what? This
depends on what Business decides.

To put it in simple terms databases can be
recovered according to one of two basic
policies:

• Recover as it was on last known full
backup.

• Point-in-time recovery.

Picture this scenario: Imagine a database
supporting a reporting application, this
particular database gets fresh data once a
week so… what would be a reasonable
backup/recovery strategy?

A reasonable backup/recovery strategy would be to take a full consistent backup of the database once a week just after it gets fresh data. Then, if something really bad happens, database can be recovered as it was after the last... or the previous data refresh.

Now picture this other scenario: Imagine a database that is supporting financial real-time transactions when something bad happens. Do you think Business would be thrilled if DBA says 'oh yeah, we can recover as it was last Saturday at noon'? I do not think so; Business will ask to recover until the last transaction or until a specific point-in-time like today at 3:43PM GMT

Depending of Business needs DBAs have to develop, implement and monitor a Backup strategy that suits the needs of the company. Setting up the right backup strategy usually involves customizing settings at database level and developing, deploying and scheduling the processes that take the actual backups.

| | |
|---|---|
| *Aha!* | *DBAs are responsible for backup strategy as well as quality of backup execution no matter if backups are physically handled by a different organization; no excuses!* |

## Database Performance

### *What's included in Performance?*

[JasonQ] how does the performance part work?
[oldDBA] Here is where the fun begins...

DBAs are responsible for overall performance of the database; that includes how the hosting computer performs, how the database performs and how the code hitting the database performs.

It is interesting to note DBAs only own the database, hosting computer is owned by System administrators and code is owned by Developers. Nevertheless, if any of those components underperforms, the Business diagnostic would be "the database is slow".

DBAs work on database performance in four different ways, which are:

- Before database goes into production, by designing and physically implementing a database for optimal performance.

- In a collaborative way by assisting and advising Development team about how to write better performing code.

- In a proactive way by monitoring the performance of a database already in production.

- In a reactive way when bad performance is detected either by DBAs, Users or Developers.

Having said that, overall performance depends on several items, including:

- The raw power and setup of the hosting computer. Usually measured in number of processors, speed of the processors and quantity of memory.

- Resource competition at hosting computer level e.g. is the hosting computer exclusively dedicated to the target database or are there other databases, applications, or whatever else running on that computer?

- I/O contention. Is storage subsystem providing the throughput the database requires? Are there any I/O bottlenecks?

- Network contention. Is network providing the throughput the database requires?

- Database design. Was the database properly designed?

- Database setup. Is the database configured to perform properly?

- Database maintenance. Is database properly maintained? Are storage fragmentation, indexes, performance statistics, etc. monitored and kept in reasonable condition?

- Quality of the code. Is the code designed and fine tuned to perform properly?

## *Measuring Performance*

[JasonQ] That's very interesting but…
[JasonQ] how do you measure performance?
[JasonQ] how can you tell if performance is good?
[oldDBA] You just touched a very sensitive point…
[oldDBA] Answer is… SLA ☺

Actually, the issue of measuring performance is a very sensitive one. No day goes by without a user in some place saying "database is slow" meaning database is performing poorly.

The question DBA asks in his/her mind is: performing poorly compared to what?

Unfortunately in some organizations there is not such thing as "compared to what" because there are not metrics to compare with. A DBA in such situation is most probably an unhappy DBA working in an unhappy organization.

SLAs are needed to measure performance. A good example of SLA for an airline reservations system would be... once the customer hits <enter> after selecting departure and arrival airports, number of travelers and dates – the system must respond in three seconds.

The above mentioned SLA includes a series of elements including Application, Network and Database. If that is the agreed SLA then DBA knows that the query that retrieves that information must take less than three seconds.

If after achieving SLA performance, meaning working for a while consistently achieving SLA levels, one day the affected query consistently goes beyond three seconds, that means something is wrong and has to be addressed.

In some cases imagination is needed and there is no doubt that it is physically impossible to set an SLA for every single query, but here comes the criticality principle: an SLA has to be set for what is critical.

This way, in an organization that measures database performance based on SLAs the Business wouldn't say "database is slow", Business would report "reservation query is under performing, it is consistently taking over three seconds" which is the agreed SLA.

There is no discussion, no perception, no interpretation, just the clear cut fact that the offending query is performing over SLA: the issue has to be identified and fixed.

| | |
|---|---|
| **Aha!** | *An organization that is serious about database performance always creates metrics in the form of SLA for critical processes or queries!* |

# Database Security

## *What is Database Security?*

[JasonQ] what's involved in security?
[oldDBA] okay... let me tell you...

As already stated, DBAs are responsible for database security.

In simple terms, database security can be defined as ensuring only authorized people have the ability to "see" the data and, only authorized people have the ability to "modify" the data. In this context, "modify the data" means having the ability of adding new data, altering already existing data or destroying data.

Please note that there is a distinction between people authorized to "see" the data and people authorized to "modify" the data. Moreover, most of the time not all people authorized to "see" data are authorized to "see" all the data.

[JasonQ] mmhh... how's that?
[oldDBA] picture this...
[oldDBA] HHRR & Payroll database... includes names, addresses, SSN, salaries, etc.
[oldDBA] ...do you follow me?
[JasonQ] y
[oldDBA] Who's authorized to "modify" data?
[JasonQ] Somebody in HHRR, is that correct?
[oldDBA] Yes! ... Who's authorized to "see" data?
[JasonQ] Everybody?
[oldDBA] Yes and No ☺
[JasonQ] How is that?
[oldDBA] You don't want everybody seeing your SSN and Salary, don't you?
[JasonQ] nah...
[oldDBA] but... you wouldn't mind if everybody can see your office phone number
[oldDBA] so... not everybody that can "see" data is authorized to "see" all the data
[JasonQ] Got it... how do you do that?

## Security Policies

Security is handled by defining and enforcing Security Policies. Security Policies are negotiated with both the Business – who knows who should have access to what and,

Auditors – who will bless the policies and make sure they are in accordance with the standards the organization needs to comply.

Usually, individual users are grouped in roles or profiles that grant similar privileges to all the users included in such role or profile.

This is done to ease the pain of administering security. Picture this scenario: the accounting department of an organization has forty-three associates that should have access to "see" the General Ledger's data; you have two ways to accomplish this:

- Individually grant the necessary privileges to those forty-three associates, then prepare yourself to maintain all those records as time goes on, or

- Grant the necessary privileges to a role or profile and then link the associates to that role or profile so they will inherit the privileges! In the future, if some privilege has to be added or revoked, you just have to deal with the appropriate role or profile.

Other than granting access to users, an equally important part of Security Policies deal with how passwords are managed. In regards to password management – just to mention a few, the most common attributes to be defined and enforced are:

- **Expiration**. Defines for how long a password can be used before it has to be changed; e.g. 90 days.

- **Format**. Defines how complex a password should be, how many characters, what kind of characters.

- **Invalid attempts**. How many times the system would allow a user to try an invalid password before locking the account.

| | |
|---|---|
| **Aha!** | *Database security involves both deciding and enforcing who can "see" and who can "modify" data as well as password management!* |

| | |
|---|---|
| **D B A corner** | *When possible, favor granting privileges through roles rather than granting privileges to specific user accounts.* *Views are your best friend when segmenting access to certain columns ;)* |

# Chapter 4

# Rules a DBA (Should) Follow

## Chapter 4 - Road Map

- Looking into how DBAs do what they do.

- Learn the set of rules DBAs (should) follow.

# Chapter 4

## Rules a DBA (Should) Follow

"Where the secrets of what a DBA does are explained in the form of a set of rules"

## Rules and Best Practices

[JasonQ] Are there any best practices a DBA follows?
[JasonQ] rules?
[oldDBA] oh yeah… books full of those
[oldDBA] I have my own summary, like a cheat sheet…
[oldDBA] wanna know?
[JasonQ] pls?

Over the years DBA learns a set of rules, sometimes learning comes from reading, appropriate training or coaching, other times learning comes the hard way. Here are the rules I personally follow –most of the time.

# Rules Defining DBA Responsibilities

## *Rule #1 –*

## *DBA owns structure but neither data nor code.*

DBA is responsible for the database as a whole but the DBA owns neither the data nor the code.

Data is owned by users, this includes the quality of the data meaning DBA should not be blamed if there is bad data in the database. Both, good and bad data come from one of two sources, Users and Code e.g. programs. Bad data means either a user error or a program error.

Code is owned by developers. Only Developers are allowed to touch and alter the code but either QA or Users – at the end of the day, are the ones that would test and certify that the code works properly.

## Rule #2 –

## DBA is responsible for database integrity

DBAs are responsible for database integrity as a whole; this means DBAs are responsible for integrity at both the logical and physical levels.

On the logical level – depending on Business specifications, database includes three levels of integrity, which are: Entity, Domain and Referential.

On the physical level DBAs are responsible for ensuring a consistent, not corrupted version of physical data files is available. See backup and recovery strategy.

## Rule #3 –

## DBA is responsible for database availability.

DBAs are responsible for keeping databases available to the user community matching, at least, the threshold specified in the specific Service Level Agreement for each particular database.

*Available* in this context means that users and applications are able to connect to the database and conduct business as expected.

## *Rule #4 –*

## *DBA is responsible for database recoverability*

DBAs are responsible for ensuring database can be recovered in the event of something going wrong. Let me be clear on this, DBA is responsible even if actual backup processes are executed by another department or external service provider.

In this context the phrase "*something going wrong*" could mean logical data corruption caused either by human or application error or physical data corruption caused by other causes like errors detected on the storage devices.

## *Rule #5 –*

## *DBA is responsible for database performance*

DBAs are responsible for overall database performance which includes not only database setup and monitoring but also monitoring the hosting computer and the quality of the code. This requires working closely to System administrators and Developers.

## Rule #6 –

## DBA is responsible for database security

DBAs are responsible for the security of the database as a whole. This includes enforcing security policies that would force users to change passwords after some period of time, expire passwords that are not longer in use, protect super user passwords to prevent them from falling in the hands of unauthorized people, etc.

## Rule #7 –

## The Gravity Rule

Sooner or later everything will fall down to the DBA desk. Gravity does it.

In terms of criticality, the most massive elements in an IT/IS environment are the databases. All other IT elements orbit around the databases. Therefore, when a problem spins out from any of the orbiting elements – it could be a storage issue, it could be a data issue or any other issue you can think about – the issue will follow the laws of gravity and fall down to the center, right on the DBA desk.

# The Three Steps Rule of Priorities

## *Rule #10 –*

## *The three steps rule of priorities.*

- First, database has to be up and available.

- Second, database has to be recoverable.

- Third, database has to perform nicely.

# The Production Rules

## *The Brain-Blood Barrier Analogy*

Please, allow me an analogy. The human body can be seen as the interaction of several systems or environments, each one of them doing some kind of processing.

Arguable the most critical system in our body is the brain plus the spinal cord. Circulation of blood and fluids going into the brain is protected by which is called the brain-blood barrier which scrutinizes what goes into that critical system stopping unwanted elements.

The blood-brain barrier stands in between the most critical environment – the brain and the other environments of the body with the final intend of protecting what is critical.

Production rules intend to apply the same concept creating a barrier to isolate as much as possible the database's most critical environment. E.g. protecting the production environment from Test and Development environments by scrutinizing what goes into production and by making sure only wanted elements go into what is most critical.

## Rule #20 –

### The Production Barrier, in General.

Nothing goes into Production if it was not tested and approved by somebody with the authority to ask for a production change.

Production changes must always be formally documented, the documentation process should allow to track back any and all production changes to its specific origin.

## Rule #21 –

### The Production Barrier, about Data.

DBA does not touch data; if DBA is asked to run a DML query, that specific DML must be at least approved by Development and Users – ideally provided by Developer, tested and approved by User.

## *Rule #22 –*

## *The Production Barrier, about Code.*

DBA does not touch backend code; requests to touch code in production environment – usually following a code promotion protocol, must be originated by Development team, tested and approved by somebody with the authority to ask for a production change in the Business side.

## *Rule #23 –*

## *The Production Barrier, Documentation.*

Production changes must leave behind a paper trail. All and any changes to the production environment must be documented. No change would never ever be done over a phone call, water cooler conversation or any other kind of undocumented interaction.

If the organization has a "*ticketing*" system, use it, if a ticketing system is not available, make sure you develop a protocol and consistently follow it. Always make sure the change is approved by somebody with the authority to do it.

# The Connections Rules

## *Rule #30 –*

### *The connections rule.*

When working on a Production database, DBAs must have no connections open against any non-production database.

When working on a non-Production database DBA must have no connections open against any Production database.

Following this simple two parts rule keeps databases healthy and DBA paychecks coming in, not to mention that helps achieving uptime SLA.

# The Monitoring Rules

## *Rule #40 –*

### *The Monitoring Rules, in General.*

DBA must know on the top of her/his head the current status of all critical production databases under her/his control – no excuses.

Other than during a catastrophic event DBA should never be taken by surprise by anything happening in her/his core responsibility databases.

## *Rule #41 –*

## *The Monitoring Rules, What to Monitor.*

Pro-actively monitor Alert logs, Space and Performance, then take action to keep alert logs clean, comfortable space allocation and reasonable performance level.

# The Design Rules

Design rules are mostly intended for DBA, Developers and other IT professionals' audience that have a vested interest in this matter, but it does not hurt if you are neither of these and decides to stay.

Please be aware that rule #50 may sound a little cryptic because it is written in Dbaish but you would either way enjoy rules #51 and #52.

## *Rule #50 –*

## *About Data Normalization*

- **50.a)** For OLTP use 3NF design.
- **50.b)** For DSS allow some degree of de-normalization.

- **50.c)** For Data Warehousing –special case of DSS rely on dimensional design.

## Rule #51 –

### About Granularity

The more ambiguous and uncertain the business definitions and requirements are, the more granular –detailed information the system has to store.

## Rule #52 –

### About Scalability

As a rule of thumbs, always take into consideration that in the database world size matters. The Larger the Database the larger the impact scalability issues will have.

If you have in your hands a small database, performance perception will be most likely acceptable no matter how poorly designed was that database and how poorly written were the queries.

On the other hand, if you have in your hands a large or very large database, as data volume goes up scalability issues will start to be more apparent until probably become your number one concern.

Allow me to illustrate scalability issues using a non-database example.

Here is the scenario. Your job is to sit down at 9:00AM and start sending pre-formatted emails to a list of addresses that your boss prepares for you the night before; you get the list in the form or an address book.

Designed process is pretty straight forward, it goes like this:

[You] select the first non-processed address from address book.

[You] go to your boss' office to ask for final approval for that particular address.

[Your boss] checks in a master list that he/she has built by adding the addresses of the day to an original list. Please note that this list keeps growing each day by the number of addresses added in that particular day. Eventually your boss finds the address in the master list and gives you final approval.

[You] go back to your desk, press <enter> and starts again until the list of addresses in your address book gets exhausted.

Piece of cake, huh?

The question is: Is this process scalable?

Taking into consideration that you get anything in between five to ten addresses a day, ask yourself how this process will work during the first two or three days. It looks to me it will work just fine; everything will be done in about five minutes at most!

Now, ask yourself how will that process work after six months? At that time your boss' master list will have approximately one thousand addresses. Remember? Your boss builds the master list by adding each day the new set of addresses to the same old master list.

It is clear that working with a one thousand entries list will be a little tricky and time consuming; you go there looking for approval then your boss has to check the list looking for the specific address you are asking to get a green light... task gets more and more time consuming as the master list grows.

Bottom line: this process is not scalable – it looks good when data volume in the master list is low, but as data volume increases overall performance decreases until making the process unbearable.

In the database world we would say that the specific process is not scalable, it was not designed and fine tuned to perform well when data volume goes up.

What can be done? There are a number of alternatives.

Perhaps your boss can keep the master list alphabetically ordered, even with an index to ease the pain of searching it from top to bottom each time you get there.

Perhaps your boss can use a shorter version of the master list for approval purposes – like a weekly list, that would be much more manageable.

Perhaps your boss can just add a "final approval" checkbox on the small list he/she sends to you every single day and avoid the recurrent "final approval" trip all together.

[JasonQ] I see...
[JasonQ] It was performing badly all the time but...
[JasonQ] nobody noticed when master list was short
[oldDBA] Exactly!

Bottom line is: databases should be designed to perform well when data volume increases;

queries should be written to perform well when data volume increases.

**D B A corner**

*As you –DBA already figure it out the example above shows how a poor performing inline view can hide for a while then hit when data volume goes up.*

*If possible, avoid use of inline views. If inline view cannot be avoided be sure inline view is scalable ;)*

## The Last Line of Defense Rule

### *Rule #60 –*

### *The Last Line of Defense Concept.*

This is a very important rule and the reason why this rule gets its own section.

DBAs are the last line of defense, whatever goes beyond DBAs will have an effect on databases, therefore will affect applications which then will have an effect on the business of the company or organization.

DBAs are expected to scrutinize every single change to production and make sure all protocols and rules are followed and authorizations are in place before doing anything affecting production.

## The Change Control Rules

### *Rule #70 –*

### *No Request, No Change.*

DBA only makes a change if a properly authorized request is received; if somebody wants a change then that somebody has to open a Request and get it authorized.

This applies to all database changes. The most usual kinds of changes a DBA performs are:

- Create new objects like a new table or index.

- Alter an existing object like adding a new column to an existing table.

- Promoting code from one environment to the next – see three tier model – like taking a new piece of code a developer has been working on in Development environment and create it or replace it on a Test environment.

- Executing a developer provided script.

Please note that DBA may initiate a Change Control Request to apply configuration changes, add storage space and activities of the sort; if the change has the potential of affecting either availability or performance, that change must be coordinated with and approved by Business.

## *Rule #71 –*

## *Script all Changes.*

All changes must be scripted; no change should be made using a GUI tool – ever.

Scripting a change allows repeating the operation again in the very same way; saving the script as part of the change documentation shows exactly what was done.

When making a change in the Production environment DBA should use the same script that was successfully applied to Test environment.

## *Rule #72 –*

## *Save all Logs.*

When applying a change, resulting log must be saved as part of the documentation of the change alongside with the script —see Rule #71

By saving both the script and the log as part of the documentation of the change, DBA ensures that Auditors, other DBAs and any other interested party will have access to both what the change intended to accomplish and what really happened during the change.

| | *I am a first hand witness of the importance of rules #70, #71 and #72.* |
|---|---|
| **D B A corner** | *Following them have saved my job more than once ;)* |

## Rule #73 –

## Enforce at the Source.

Fix it when in development – when possible.

On Chapter 5 we will address how the three tier infrastructure model applies to a database environment. At this point is more than enough to perceive the database environment as a three stories building serviced by an escalator – which is nothing but the change control management procedures that handle how changes move from one environment to the next.

Development is at the ground floor, each time somebody puts something in the escalator, sooner or later that something – a piece of code, a change to a table structure, etc. – would certainly reach the Test environment in the first floor and sometime later the Production environment in the second floor.

The closer to the Production environment things get, the more difficult is to change them. DBA should do her/his best to detect changes affecting design or code that might have a negative impact on the database, the sooner as possible.

The ideal situation is to detect and fix issues while still on the development environment, otherwise somebody is going to say something on the line of "it is too late to change the approach, we will have to live with it".

The problem is that the unfixed issue may, most likely, impact performance or availability which are two of DBA's responsibilities.

# The Security Rules

## *Rule #80 –*

## *Grant Privileges through Roles*

When possible, grant privileges through roles; avoid granting privileges to specific user accounts.

By doing this, security administration will be less painful and, you will make auditors happy.

## *Rule #81 –*

## *Secure Super User Passwords*

Never ever keep the default password on any system –super user account.

Most system accounts have DBA privileges or close to DBA privileges, default passwords are widely documented therefore a default password on any of these accounts is like leaving the door of your house wide open.

**D B A corner**

*This is a pretty easy catch for Auditors.*

*Lets avoid leaving default passwords on system accounts and make them work a little harder ;)*

## *Rule #82 –*

## *No Authorization, No Security Change*

Security is a serious matter then please allow me customize Rule #70 specifically to address security.

Any and all security changes must be done after proper request and authorization. Security changes must leave a paper trail and be documented.

*Security changes include:*

- Creating new accounts.
- Resetting password on existing accounts.
- Granting or revoking privileges to/from a role or account.
- Adding or removing accounts to/from a role.
- Altering password management setup.

# The People Skills Rules

The set of rules below are not technical but people skills related. They address how to better communicate and cultivate a positive relationship with other people. Over the years I learned the hard way that an old friend of mine was spot-on when he said:

- It is not enough to be good; you also have to look good.

- Trouble people are most likely going to stay around forever; you have to find a way to work with them.

## *Rule #90 –*

## *Be the Can-Do Person*

No matter what, always smile, have a positive attitude and let other people know you are there to help and you will be glad to help them.

Do your best to work issues out, politely stick to procedures and, be firm but courteous.

Be the person everybody wants to work with, do not look for a culprit and, always focus in solving the problem.

**D B A corner**

*The can-do attitude produces magical results.*

*In time, users and developers will come to you as soon as they feel something is off, they will be more candid and, chances are problems will be solved in a smoother and civil way ;)*

## Rule #91 –

### Avoid Speaking Dbaish

When working with non DBA avoid speaking Dbaish as much as possible. Communicate in the "*language*" of your interlocutors.

Avoid being perceived as pretentious.

## Rule #92 –

### Be Prepared to Explain it One More Time

Always be prepared to explain it – whatever the message you are trying to convey – one more time.

The burden of communication rests on the person attempting to convey a message. If the message is not understood you have to try again, smile and explain it one more time in a different way.

## Rule #93 –

### The Agreement Rule

It is not an unseen event that at the end of a meeting – *meeting* in this context means any gathering of two or more people, physically or virtually to discuss an issue and make a decision about it – participants happily go back to their desks... every one of them with a different understanding about what the outcome was.

Always end a meeting by saying: "so we agree that < list here everything you think was the out-come of the meeting >. Is that correct?"

More often than expected you may find not everybody was clear about the outcome. If this is the case smile, initiate a second round and, do not forget to apply rules #90 and #92.

**D B A corner**

*As you can see the above mentioned "rules" look like simple "common sense".*

*The trick is to apply "common sense" in an organized way so to ensure no self inflicted wounds happen ;)*

# Chapter 5

# How is the Database Environment Organized?

Chapter 5 - Road Map

- Looking at the infrastructure behind DBA activity.

- Learn about infrastructure.

- Learn about DBA specialization.

Chapter 5

How is the Database Environment
Organized?

"Where Jason show interest in knowing
the mechanics of the database
environment"

## What is there other than Production?

[JasonQ] that's an interesting set of rules
[oldDBA] glad you like them
[JasonQ] I can see several rules about production...
[JasonQ] what else is out there?
[oldDBA] Development, Test, UAT, QA, Staging...
[oldDBA] ...it depends on the organization
[JasonQ] could you be a little more specific?
[oldDBA] sure, let me share with you a proven
infrastructure model...

Different organizations structure the database environment in different ways. On despite of the adopted model, the ultimate idea is to –at least separate Development from Production.

Depending on the specific organization and the criticality of the specific database you can find variations going from a simple Development/ Production environment to complex models adding other intermediate levels of isolation.

## The Three Tier Model

The three tier model is a battle tested infrastructure model that applies not only to the database but is also useful as a framework for software development, testing and deployment, including activities from DBA, Development team and User community.

This model is designed to support activities during the three major phases of an Information Systems project, which are:

- Development,
- Test and,
- Production.

The underlying idea is to isolate different environments to support each one of those phases; it allows for conducting development in an environment that would affect neither Testing nor Production, conducting testing in an environment that would affect neither Development nor Production and operate the Production environment with interference neither from Development nor from Testing.

## *The Ideal Three Tier Infrastructure*

The ideal three tier infrastructure in regards to the database environment should include one dedicated host computer for each environment e.g. Development, Test –also known as UAT for **U**ser **A**cceptance **T**esting and, Production.

Please note that in this context the term host computer could either be a physical dedicated computer, a logical partition or virtual machine (of a single computer), a cluster, or a virtualized computer running either in a virtual server or cloud alike infrastructure.

The objective of the three tier infrastructure model is to attain absolute independence and isolation among the three environments e.g. development, test and production.

## *Development Environment*

- **Usage**:

  In the three tier infrastructure model the Development environment is the place where development effort takes place; neither user testing nor production activities should be allowed in a development environment.

- **Size**:

  Depending on certain circumstances, Development environment would be anything from 5% to 20% of the expected size of the Production environment. Size includes both space and processing power.

- **Who controls the environment**:

  Shared control between Developers and DBAs.

  Developers control their own private areas where they are the master and commander.

  DBAs control the operational area where developers conduct basic integration tests.

Developers should not have privileges to create or alter objects in the operational area; all objects in this area should be created and altered by DBAs as a response to a Developer's request.

- **Security**:

  In the development environment, developers are usually expected to have full control of their own private working areas, they also should have user-community alike privileges on the operational area so to allow initial integration testing.

  None or just a few selected users should be allowed into development environment and in that case only on the operational area, never on developer's private working areas

## *Test Environment*

- **Usage**:

  This is the place where users conduct testing; neither development nor production activity should be allowed in test environment.

- **Size**:

  Ideally this environment should have the same storage size as Production while it may have just a token of what Production has in terms of processing power and memory; this is because Test environment should allow to test on production alike data but just a few users are expected to have access to it.

- **Who controls the environment**:

  DBAs control Test environment.

  Developers must not have any development related privileges on Test environment; all objects are created and altered by DBAs responding to a request from the head of the Development department.

- **Security**:

  Test environment in a fully fleshed three tier model infrastructure is expected to have an image of production data – not only in volume but also in content. This is a very important concept to have in mind because that means it should be secured in the same way as is production.

  A selected group of members of the user community – the beta testers, should have access to the Test environment mirroring the privileges they have in the production environment.

Usually developers are allowed to have accounts with user access to the environment but never ever they should have "developer" alike privileges.

Password management including password expiration policies should be enforced as it happens in production.

## *Production Environment*

- **Usage**:

  The place where Production happens. Neither Testing nor Development allowed.

- **Size**:

  As large as Production activity requires.

- **Who controls the environment**:

  DBAs control Production environment.

  Developers should not have any development related privileges on Production environment; all objects should be created and altered by DBAs responding to a request from the head of the Development department authorized by the head of the User community that owns the particular database.

- **Security**:

    This is Production environment, it should be secured. Please see Chapter 3, Database Security.

    In a nutshell, developers should have no access at all to Production environment, Users should have access as agreed with the Business and all security policies should be established and enforced.

# DBA Internal Organization

[JasonQ] Not sure why, but I like the three tier model
[oldDBA] good
[JasonQ] How about the people...
[JasonQ] meaning...
[JasonQ] how are DBA human resources organized
[oldDBA] That depends on too many factors
[oldDBA] let me explain...

## *In General*

Internal organization of DBAs depends on many factors including the size of the organization, the number and size of the databases, the variety of database technology vendors and, how mature and stable the databases are. There are just too many of them to mention them all.

## *Expertise Level*

It is not possible to avoid saying DBAs come in three expertise levels which are: Junior (entry level), Intermediate and Senior.

The previous statement is aligned with what we have already established: in the DBA world experience matters.

What may come as a surprise is that experience matters at two different levels: the first one is the level of mastering a DBA has on a specific platform like Oracle, IBM-DB2, SQL Server, etc. and, the second one is the level of mastering the DBA has in regards to the databases of the host organization.

To put it in simple terms, a DBA who is an absolute genius on a specific technology may struggle at the time of supporting a specific database because he/she may not know how that specific database works, how it was designed, how it is hit by the application and users, who owns the database, etc.

Taking into consideration that takes years of technical training and hands-on experience to master a specific technology e.g. Oracle, IBM-DB2, SQL Server, etc. and, also takes years of day-by-day contact with a specific database to master how it works, organizations should try to retain good DBAs and have as less rotation as possible in that department.

## DBA Functions

There are a number of different DBA functions hidden under the DBA label. Most DBAs cover more than one of those functions. Moreover, function titles may vary from organization to organization as well as the fine grain responsibilities of each one.

In my mind, DBA functions can be easily cataloged as follows: Production support DBA, Development DBA, Database architect.

## Production Support DBA

As Pacific Salmon is the most common kind of Salmon, Production Support DBA is the most common kind of DBA. Most of the time people use the term DBA to refer to a Production Support DBA.

Production Support DBAs are the ones assigned to make sure existing databases have no Integrity issues and are Available, Recoverable, Performing well and Secure.

[JasonQ] aren't those the responsibilities of a DBA?
[oldDBA] exactly!... you are paying attention

Most of the working hours of a Production Support DBA are spent in proactive monitoring, maintenance and problem troubleshooting and resolution.

[JasonQ] maintenance? What's that?

*Maintenance* in this context means two different things, maintain the actual databases and maintain the database software – not what is developed in house but the vendor's software engine that makes the database work.

Database maintenance includes:

- Reorganizing tables and indexes,
- Administering space and,

- Applying software patches or updates.

Keeping databases operational is not an easy task, critical databases have SLAs asking for 24 by 7 availability. That means that most Production Support DBAs carry pagers and are part of 24 by 7 on-call rotations.

## Development Support DBA

Some organizations have DBAs assigned full time to Development Support activities, in other organizations Senior Level DBAs cover this function part time.

In a perfect world, no software development project should proceed if there is no Development Support DBA as part of the team.

A Development Support DBA is the one that would ensure code is written in a way that takes advantage of the way the database is designed and the features of the chosen technology.

Development Support DBA also set coding standards, writes back-end code and, coaches and mentors software developers.

Finally, Development Support DBA should be able to work on tactical database design, probably not designing the overall structure but certainly adding or improving specific modules.

## Database Architect

This function is usually reserved for a true Senior Level DBA who also masters other skills like Functional Analysis and Data Modeling. At this level that person is usually well acquainted with Systems and Storage side technologies.

A big plus is for a Database Architect to have a business perspective; this would be helpful to better understand how databases support the business of the host organization.

Database Architect should be involved every time a new database is planned and designed, also each time the functionality of an existent database is being expanded.

The Database Architect is the final responsible for strategic Database design, systems integration and capacity planning.

| Aha! | It turns out there are several flavors of DBA, each one of them with specific responsibilities and skills set! |
| --- | --- |

# Chapter 6

# With whom does a DBA Interact?

## Chapter 6 - Road Map

- Looking into people around DBA activity.

- Learn about the roles of the people DBAs interact with, how those roles relate to DBA activities.

Chapter 6

With whom does a DBA Interact?

"Where Jason comes to understand
DBAs do not work in isolation"

## Do DBAs Work in Isolation?

[JasonQ] ... do you have contact with other
departments?
[JasonQ] or do you work on your own?
[JasonQ] with whom in the organization a DBA works?
[oldDBA] well, well... this may come as a surprise...
[oldDBA] DBA works with everybody in the
organization...
[oldDBA] let me show you...

Some of my acquaintances still think of DBAs
as people working in an isolated dungeon,

performing strange rituals to keep databases alive – I have to agree I can picture a couple of my former co-workers in the middle of the night wearing a black cloak and hood, their faces barely visible on the greenish dim glow of an old IBM 3278 terminal murmuring *"be sargable... be sargable..."* when working in a nasty query but, what really happens in real world is the absolute opposite; DBA activity touches every single aspect of the IT environment and beyond.

## Working with Systems Administrators

DBAs work with Systems administrators because databases are sitting on a computer. DBA depends on Systems administrators to have a suitable platform all the way from hardware to the Operating System; and that task is Systems administrator's responsibility.

Smart DBAs learn to build a comfortable and cooperative relationship with System administrators; after all, members of those two teams will be working together during those late night and weekend maintenance windows.

## Working with Network Engineers

DBAs work with Network engineers because clients –people and applications, are connecting to the databases through the Network.

DBAs also rely on the network for data replication, either when it is done for operational or for business continuity purposes.

Network engineers, either working as part of a Systems Administration team or as part of their own Networking team, are responsible for network connectivity.

# Working with Storage Administrators

Medium to large environments rely on SAN and NAS storage solutions that are external to the actual computers. The administration of such storage solutions is responsibility of Storage administrators, either working as part of a Systems Administration team or as part of their own Storage team

Databases are sitting on storage, the very definition of a database points to a set of files in a storage device, therefore DBA works with Storage administrators not only in the physical layout of a database but also in monitoring performance and troubleshooting I/O bottlenecks.

## Working with Backup Team

One of DBA responsibilities is "database recoverability", meaning that DBA must ensure databases can be recovered in case something goes wrong. This requires having proper Backup/ Recovery policies and processes in place.

In medium to large environments backups are centralized with a specific Data compliance / Backup team in charge of the operation of the backup processes. However, responsibility for those backups is still on the desk of DBA, hence DBA works closely with Data compliance / Backup team to ensure databases are recoverable.

## Working with Development Team

Development teams, also known as Applications teams, are the owners of the code, a.k.a. programs.

Code that hit a database comes in two flavors: back-end and front-end code. Back-end code is the one residing in the database in the form of stored procedures, functions, triggers, etc. while front-end code is the code residing outside the database like in an application or web server.

DBAs and Developers work pretty closely.

Developers rely on DBAs to make changes to database structures and also to move code up the ladder from the Development environment all the way to Production.

DBAs also act as advisors working in poor performing queries and fine tuning processes.

In a perfect world, no query should be executed against production if not approved by DBA. This statement used to hold true during the mainframe era; nowadays in the era of rapid development and ad-hoc queries more and more poor performing pieces of code can be seen happily hitting databases all around.

In my experience few organizations are still adamant of this old principle especially when talking about critical databases.

## Working with Project Managers

DBAs – particularly Senior DBAs, are usually involved in large projects.

Projects –any organized effort taking 200 or more hours of labor, usually requires having a Project Manager running the show.

Project Managers are in general well organized people, something most DBAs like and appreciate, therefore most of the time Project Managers and DBA team up in a seamless way.

From the DBA point of view nothing beats to have a good Project Manager assigned to a complex project; that is a guarantee DBA will be able to focus in what DBA does best letting the Project Manager deal with other teams and politics.

## Working with User Community

The average DBA seldom works with final users; there is a reason for this. A medium size database in a medium size company may have hundreds or even thousands of individual users, the potential number of calls to DBA would be large enough to prevent DBA from doing what it does best, which is deal with databases.

If a user has connectivity or authentication issues the user should contact help-desk. Help desk should have protocols in place to help users solve simple connectivity and authentication issues including password resetting.

If a user has application issues, or has reasons to believe something is wrong with the data, the user should contact the Development team. Development team should have the ability to troubleshoot the issue and determine if the user is facing a real problem or if the issue is due to operational causes.

Help desk and Development team should be tier one support for the user community; if either Help desk or Development team feel DBA should be involved they are the ones that would get in touch with DBA.

# Working with Auditors

At this point in the book you already know DBAs are responsible for database Integrity, Availability, Recoverability, Performance and Security. Note that not less than four out of the abovementioned five items are usually audited; auditors will sooner or later go after the policies and processes used to deal with database Integrity, Availability, Recoverability and Security – in some cases they might also be interested in Performance.

The job of the auditor is to ask questions. The easiest way to deal with auditors and have a positive relationship with them is to be prepared, answer the questions and work together in any items that might need improvement.

| | |
|---|---|
| **Aha!** | *It turns out DBA has to interact with a lot of people, better check the "people skills" of the next DBA candidate.* |

# Chapter 7

# Where do Database Administrators Come From?

## Chapter 7 - Road Map

- Looking into the making of a DBA.

- Learn about DBA skills, education and training.

- Learn about the road to a DBA position.

- Experience vs. Certifications.

Chapter 7

Where do Database Administrators
Come From?

"Where Jason finds out where Database
Administrators come from"

## The Making of a DBA

[oldDBA] so... are you getting a picture?
[JasonQ] interesting, I have to say.
[JasonQ] how do you become a DBA?
[JasonQ] What do you study? ... How does it work?
[oldDBA] oh... you are gonna love this one ☺

It may surprise you that it is highly unusual for
a DBA to initiate her or his career as a DBA;
most of the time the DBA-to-be transitions to a

DBA position after working for a while in other IT/IS positions.

There are reasons for this to happen, lets take a look at the skills you expect to see in a DBA; you may be surprised most of the skills listed below are not technical skills per-se.

## Attention to Detail

DBAs are expected to be detail oriented people.

DBA activities in general require having the ability to troubleshoot, to figure out solutions then to put together a plan of action involving, in general, a series of steps. Needless to say, DBAs have to be aware of any issues during such processes; the ability and predisposition to check and understand logs is a must have.

Attention to detail is a skill you may expect to see in a programmer or project manager.

## Broad Vision

DBAs –especially Senior DBAs are expected to have broad vision.

They have to understand how a given database supports specific business applications; they have to understand how different databases in the organization work together, they have to be aware of the overall implications of any change made on any specific database.

Broad vision is the kind of skill you would expect to see in a Functional Analyst or Systems Analyst. It should not come as a surprise that many heavy-weights; really good at database design DBAs have a Functional Analyst or Systems Analyst background.

## Highly Organized

DBAs are expected to be organized people.

It is not uncommon to see DBAs working at the core of projects involving a number of interrelated, dependent tasks – in many cases involving different departments.

Such projects including but not restricted to physical deployment or a new database, application of RDBMS patches, migrations, upgrades, maintenance windows of different sorts, etc., usually require to put together a detailed timeline to organize activities that have to be completed by different people in different departments.

Since organizations usually do not assign a Project Manager for any effort of less than two hundred hours, most of those projects are actually handled by DBAs.

You may recognize that these kinds of skills are the ones you would expect to see in a Project Manager. It is not unusual to see DBAs with Project Management background.

## *Logic and Abstract Thinking*

DBAs –especially Senior DBAs are expected to be proficient at scripting on Operating System scripting language and on the flavor or SQL language supported by the RDBMS of choice.

These are nothing but programming skills you would expect to see in a programmer. This is the reason why many DBAs have a background in programming e.g. software development, software engineering.

## *Bottom Line – The DBA Path*

Nowadays most DBAs have a college degree, usually a Bachelor of Science in any IT or IS related field.

Armed with that degree and eventually some extra technical training people manage to secure some entry level position in the IT industry, at some point in time they find themselves working in a programming related position and discover databases. Some of those that feel they like or are interested in the database field, in time may press their bosses asking for responsibilities around databases, perhaps as SQL developers.

The ones lucky enough to like databases may eventually get a chance to secure a DBA entry level position then learn the secrets of the trade by formal and informal training, as well as by day-by-day hands on experience.

| **Aha!** | *A DBA position is like a highway people access after traveling other roads!* |
|---|---|

# Certifications vs. Experience

[JasonQ] You didn't mention certifications...
[JasonQ] Are there any database certifications?
[JasonQ] How they match against experience?
[oldDBA] another good topic you put your finger on.

This question brings up to the table the topic of Industry Certifications. As it happens on all IT fields, each and all RDBMS vendors offer its own version of a certification path.

An Industry Certification path is based on the idea of people getting training either formal or informal then facing and passing – or failing – a series of proctored tests.

Let me be clear on this, in my personal view Certifications are not a replacement for Experience.

Having said that I do believe certifications have value, especially at hiring time. Let me explain why.

- A candidate that got a certification shows me that she/he is serious enough to take the time to get trained then to face tests.

- The fact that a candidate got a specific certification tells me that that person had exposure to a number of specific concepts.

When hiring an entry level DBA, when two candidates have the same apparent credentials, I would certainly opt for the one with the appropriate certifications.

| **Aha!** | *Even when "experience" is what matters…*<br>*Industry certifications are a plus!* |

# Are DBA Multilingual?

[JasonQ] are DBA multilingual?
[JasonQ] how many database "languages" DBA
speaks?
[oldDBA] That's a pretty good question, let me tell you

## The Two Positions

There are two opposite positions in regards to
the level of specialization a DBA should have
in terms of database technology, e.g. how
many database technologies a DBA should
specialize on.

Let's call these two positions the one held by
"purists" and the one held by "liberals".

Purists argue that any specific database
technology e.g. Oracle, DB2, SQL Server, etc.
is so broad and deep that DBAs should focus
on one of them and, master it to its finest
grain.

On the other hand Liberals argue that a DBA should gain working knowledge of two, maybe more, technologies, making her/him more valuable for the organization and also broadening the job market at the time of looking for new job opportunities.

Which one is the correct one?

I would say both positions carry real value; like in quantum physics both are correct.

Let me attempt to clarify this position by saying that it is not uncommon to see organizations running databases in more than one technology, in my particular case the organization I work for relies on databases running on a variety of versions of Oracle, SQL Server and Sybase.

On the one hand, I like to work in a team where one or more team members are able to cover responsibilities on more than one technology platform.

On the other hand I do appreciate the opportunity of talking with a heavy weight expert in a specific technology when I have to call – in my case – either: Oracle, Microsoft (SQL Server) or Sybase asking for help.

In my case, being myself fluent in three *human* languages I find almost natural being also fluent in Oracle and SQL Server, while having working knowledge of Sybase.

[JasonQ] What prevents you from learning, let's say Oracle
[JasonQ] then SQL Server, then DB2 and so on
[JasonQ] until mastering all of them?
[oldDBA] time does it, let me explain.

## *The Time Constraint*

There is a physical reason why you wouldn't expect a DBA to master a large number of RDBMS; the reason is that there are twenty-four hours in a day and as Peter Drucker used to say: "The supply of time is totally inelastic. No matter how high the demand, the supply will not go up".

DBAs need time to keep pace with the new features of the technology they already master as vendors keep releasing new versions. It is not that you learn let's say Oracle and you know it forever; Oracle will release new versions and you need time for that. The same happens with all technology vendors.

DBA needs time to research and test. In the DBA world the old saying "practice perfects it" applies big time.

DBA also needs time to actually do some work, the DBA's employer expects DBA to actually perform some real work other than mastering the technology.

Finally, DBA needs time and the opportunity to perform hands-on work on whatever technology or technologies she or he masters. If skills are not used, skills will be lost in a very short period of time.

| | |
|---|---|
| **Aha!** | *Even when all DBAs have the same responsibilities, since they master specific technologies like Oracle, IBM-DB2, SQL Server, etc. they will perform well only on the technologies they master!* |

# Conclusion

[JasonQ] so... do you like being a DBA?
[oldDBA]I love it! ☺
[oldDBA] DBAs are the guardians of the data, think on them as the old keepers of the fire

DBAs live in an exciting but demanding world: they work long days and nights, carry a pager; participate in on-call rotations and have a steep price to pay when errors or mistakes happen, even when the error or mistake may not be DBA's fault.

Nobody has DBAs on mind when everything goes smoothly but everybody looks at DBAs when something goes wrong.

I just love it!

# Chapter 8

# Bonus Chapter –What if?

Chapter 8 - Road Map

- Some intriguing chit-chat about parallels between nature and technology.

Chapter 8

Bonus Chapter –What if?

"Where Jason takes home something
extra to think about"

---

## Cool Down Period

We are done with the technical part of this
book but considering the colloquial style we
have relied on, let's do it the right way and
cool down before we depart.

[oldDBA] Did you get your answers?
[JasonQ] oh yes!
[JasonQ] Thanks a lot buddy… have to sign off ☺
[oldDBA] Fantastic, take this to think on it at home…

---

# What If?

What if IT technology is mimicking nature even if we are not aware of it?

[JasonQ] hit me...
[oldDBA] Have you noticed how Technology mimics Nature? Birds and planes, you know?
[oldDBA] What if our IT technology is mimicking nature even if we are not aware of it?

## *Acknowledgment*

This short chapter is loosely based on the work –soon to be published of Raquel Yosver. She has run the ideas outlined below with scholars who had not dismiss them but had given a positive feedback.

Since I personally found these ideas very exciting for say the least, let me share them with you the same way we use to end a meeting with a note in a sometimes not totally related issue.

Please take note this chapter does not intends to be a scientific paper but a water-cooler style chit-chat where two or more persons share their particular takes in a specific subject.

With no further ado allow me to outline one of these ideas which are related to database technology in particular.

---

# Sleep and Archive Logs

## *The Nature Side*

It is a well documented fact that sleep plays an important role in what some scientists call memory consolidation.

Sleep deprivation causes hallucinations – which are nothing but memory flashes, headaches, impair the ability to concentrate and think, etc., leading to what I would call a *crash* of the sleep deprived person.

## *The Technology Side*

Allow me to speak a little Oracleish to describe the database technology side even when all RDBMS have somehow alike processes.

What happens with a database that runs on archivelog mode when archive space is exhausted?

Answer: When the particular database reaches a point where cannot write the redo log buffer to disk anymore the particular database would stop working.

## *The Parallels –What if?*

What if the nature process of sleeping is actually flushing a redo log buffer? Moving data a.k.a. memories from a temporary buffer to a more permanent storage location?

Sleep deprivation would prevent the brain from accomplishing that task so the affected system, a.k.a. the sleep deprived person's brain, would come to a halt.

Have you seen what happens when a database crashes and current redo log cannot be recovered? Incomplete recovery, isn't it? Meaning the database is not able to remember what happened immediately before the crash. Not to mention non-committed transactions running at the time of the crash, which are lost forever.

Have you noticed in some accidents when a person has head trauma – the affected person may have literally crashed, that person is unable to remember what happened immediately before the crash? Is it possible that the brain processed an incomplete recovery because buffered data a.k.a.

memories got lost as a consequence of the crash?

Raised questions about those and other parallels between the solutions *nature* implements and the solutions *our technology* implements are very interesting indeed; we may have replicated –mimicked those particular features of the processes used by nature in our database technology without knowing it.

If we did in fact replicate those features, we can be very proud of our accomplishment. Our technology does not require putting the database to sleep as part of a sleep-awake serial cycle to flush the redo buffer logs; our databases are able to do it in parallel. On the other hand, when our database technology does an incomplete recovery that is the end of the road and no further recovery will be done. However, nature has showed once and again that after an incomplete recovery, that allows the affected person to be back in commission, it keeps trying and over time may be able to recover more data a.k.a. memories.

There are more intriguing ideas from where these come from, stay tuned.

# Appendix I
# Dbaish - English Dictionary

Appendix I

- Looking into technical jargon.

- Learn how to translate Dbaish to English.

# Appendix I

## Dbaish – English Dictionary

### "Where Jason finds what those Dbaish words mean..."

## When a DBA says... You should hear...

*3NF (Data modeling): See Third Normal Form.*

***Business*** *(Business owner): Refers in particular to the head of the user community that owns a particular database and in general to the individual users of that group.*

**Cluster**: *A group of resources of the same kind working together to improve availability and/or performance.*

**Code**: *Programs and scripts. Back-end code are the pieces of code residing in the database in the form of stored procedures, functions, triggers, etc. Front-end code are the pieces of code residing outside the database, usually on application servers, web servers, etc.*

**Column** *(relational theory): Vertical division of a table. In our example columns in Customers table describe each one of the attributes of "Customer" like: address, phone number, industry, etc.*

**Data modeling**: *The process of deciding how data is going to be laid out in a database. Data modeling is the direct precursor to deciding which tables have to be created as well as which columns each table should include.*

**Data Warehouse**: *A type of database designed to store large amounts of data allowing reporting and business intelligence processes rather than support any specific operational activity.*

**DBA**: *Acronym for **D**ata **B**ase **A**dministrator.*

---

**DBMS**: *Acronym for **D**ata **B**ase **M**anagement **S**ystem.*

**DDL**: *Acronym for **D**ata **D**efinition **L**anguage. A piece of code that intends to affect metadata. E.g. to alter the structure of the database by altering table structures or other object structures –like adding a column to a table.*

**DML**: *Acronym for **D**ata **M**anipulation **L**anguage. A piece of code that intends to alter data in any form like inserting, updating or deleting.*

**DSS**: *Acronym for **D**ecision **S**upport **S**ystems; refers to reporting and data warehouse databases.*

**GUI** *(GUI tool): Acronym for **G**raphic **U**ser Interface, in this specific case a piece of software designed to interact with databases.*

**Host** *(host computer): refers to the computer where the database is sitting also referred as a "box". It can be a whole physical computer, a logical partition or virtual machine of a large computer or, a virtual server.*

**IS**: *Information Systems. Usually refers to the department that, relying on Information Technology, processes data until it becomes information.*

**IT**: *Information Technology. Usually refers to the Information Technology Industry, the one that provides everything that is needed to process data.*

**Metadata**: *Data about the data. Metadata about a specific table would define the columns and other attributes of such a table.*

**Navigation** *(database navigation): The way the database architect or designer envisioned information will be related to each other usually supported by indexes and relationships in between tables. Example: Once a specific customer is selected from Customers table the user may get access (navigate) to all invoices belonging to that customer in Invoices table.*

**Non-Sargable**: *A query which is non sargable. Queries that are non-sargable are expected to perform poorly and should be prevented to be deployed in a production environment. See "sargable".*

***Normalization*** *(data modeling): Refers to a set of techniques and rules designed to model data. The most famous and widely used of the normal forms is the Third Normal Form or 3NF.*

***OLTP****: Acronym for **On Line Transaction** Processing. In our case a database supporting a real time system like an airline reservations and ticketing system.*

***Predicate*** *(predicate of a query): Conditions on the WHERE clause of a query.*

***Promotion*** *(code promotion): The process of moving code into a specific database. Usually done by extracting code from a lower environment and applying the script to a higher environment – see three tier environment.*

***Query:*** *Statement written in SQL.*

***RDBMS****: Acronym for **R**elational **D**ata **B**ase **M**anagement **S**ystem. Nowadays – arguable- all commercially viable databases are relational.*

***Replication*** *(data replication): The processes involved in replicating data from one database to another. Replication allows* for synchronizing two databases or a portion of two databases either for load balancing, reporting or business continuity purposes.

**Row** *(relational theory): Horizontal division of a table. In our example each row in Customers table describes each one of the customers.*

**Sargable***: Short for **S**earch **Arg**ument **Able**. This old jargon term means a specific query is written in a way the predicate takes advantage of overall database navigation and indexes. A sargable query is expected to be efficient.*

**SLA***: Acronym for **S**ervice **L**evel **A**greement. Probably the most important SLA for a DBA is "uptime" meaning the percentage of time a specific database is expected to be available to the user community, like 99.8% for a real-time OLTP critical database.*

**SQL***: Acronym for Structured Query Language. All modern RDBMS "talk" some flavor of SQL.*

**Sysadmin***: Short for Systems Administrator. Sysadmin are the members of the team* in charge of –at least the hardware and the operating system.

**Table** *(relational theory): A set of organized data that usually describes a set of entities of the same kind e.g. Customers table describes "customers" while Invoices table describes "invoices".*

**Third Normal Form**, *3NF (data modeling): The most widely used standard to model data and its relationships, especially for OLTP systems.*

**Three Tier Environment**: *A model that isolates Development, Test and Production in three separate environments. See Chapter 5.*

**Tuple**: *Row*

**Where** *(where clause): Section of a query where conditions are specified, also called predicate.*

CPSIA information can be obtained at www.ICGtesting.com
Printed in the USA
LVOW121850181112

307840LV00001B/63/P

# Understanding

# Database

# Administration

**Pablo Berzukov**